Written by Jared Kelner

Written by Jared Kelner
Directed by Gerry Appel

A Fearless Productions Show

2015 Thespis Theater Festival
Hudson Guild Theater
441 W. 26th Street, NY
September 17th & 18th at 6:15pm
September 20th at 8:30pm

Title: A Promise To Your Mother

Publisher: The Infinite Mind Training Group
(www.memory-trainers.com)

Playwright: Jared Kelner
(www.jaredkelner.com)

Cover Art: CORSI DESIGN
(corsi617@gmail.com)

ISBN-10: 0982655886

ISBN-13: 978-0-9826558-8-7

All rights reserved. No part of this book may be reproduced or transmitted in any form or by any means without written permission from the playwright, except for the inclusion of brief quotations in a review.

Copyright © 2015 by Jared Kelner

First Edition, 2015

Published in the United States of America

For Performance Inquires
Contact Jared Kelner
jared@jaredkelner.com

To watch a video of the original
cast performance, visit
www.jaredkelner.com

Notes from the Playwright

Love, when focused, can overcome the tragedies in life

    A PROMISE TO YOUR MOTHER explores the lives of those left in the wake of one man's heinous crimes. Malcolm made national news when a vengeance-filled father of a girl Malcolm was accused of raping, crashed his car into Malcolm's, killing Malcolm and his wife. The tragedy sparks a series of revelations that will forever entwine the lives of Malcolm's 14 year-old daughter, his twin brother, a young mother with a haunting past and her 15 year-old derelict son.

    Thank you to the Thespis Theater Festival Staff for accepting this play into the festival and providing the opportunity to share it with the world. You have all be incredibly supportive and that is greatly appreciated.

    Thank you FEARLESS PRODUCTIONS for the amazing support and generosity throughout this journey. I am humbled and honored to be connected with such a passionate and dedicated group of artists.

Notes from the Director

One person reacts to the touch of evil in their youth by spreading that evil throughout their dark, sinister life. Victim becomes demon.

Another person learns from that touch of evil in their youth and helps others suffering from similar circumstances. Victim becomes healer.

In the painful, twisted maze of A PROMISE TO YOUR MOTHER, four victims yearn for a safe place – a place to connect, to share, to trust.

As you witness their journey, consider this: What if it were you? Which road would you take?

FEARLESS PRODUCTIONS
(www.fearlessprod.com)

Fearless Productions strives to create entertaining theatrical productions that walk on the very edge of the edge, leap enthusiastically with our hearts on our sleeves, and dare to be daring. We recognize that the responsibility of true art is to firmly grasp the attention of our audience for as long as we are asking for it. We accept this challenge with the courage that only comes with doing exactly what we feel we were born to do... Simply put... Our NAME is our MISSION STATEMENT.

THE CAST

Jared Kelner (Ben/Malcolm)

Jared studied acting in CA, NY and NJ and has appeared professionally on Stage, TV and Film. Favorite roles include Alan in WHAT DO THEY BECOME?, Howard in RABBIT HOLE, George in GLENGARRY GLEN ROSS & Epstein in BILOXI BLUES. Jared recently appeared in the film MADELEINE directed by UK-Based Ollie Verschoyle. Jared is honored to have his second play brought to life by an incredible cast under the guidance of a talented and generous Director. Thank you Rachel, Kayla, Justin & Gerry for your commitment to this play. I am indebted to you all. Jared would like to thank his son and daughter for their never ending support and especially thank his wife for loving him and giving him the opportunity to spend so much time in LaLa Land. Finally, a massive Thank You for the support of Brian Remo, Kristin Barber and Kara Wilson from Fearless Productions. We are so fortunate to be part of the Fearless Productions family (jared@jaredkelner.com, www.jaredkelner.com)

THE CAST

Rachel Persenaire (Celia)

Rachel is thrilled to be a part of such a talented cast and production team for A PROMISE TO YOUR MOTHER. Rachel carries a B.A. in Theatre Arts: Acting and Directing, and an M.A. in Music and Music Education. Favorite past roles include Ann in ALL MY SONS, Karen in AUGUST: OSAGE COUNTY, Clytemnestra in THE GREEKS: THE MURDERS, and Olivia in TWELFTH NIGHT. Rachel is a vocal and piano teacher offering training in New York and New Jersey. Special thanks to Fearless Productions, Jared and Gerry, and of course, family and loved ones for their unending support and love. (racheldunwoody@mac.com)

THE CAST

Kayla Folz (Mandy)

Kayla has studied acting for the past three years at Actors Playground in Freehold NJ and has also taken a variety of acting classes in New York. Playing the character Mandy in A PROMISE TO YOUR MOTHER marks Kayla's on stage acting debut. Although this is her first stage appearance, Kayla has appeared on Dateline NBC's MY KID WOULD NEVER DO THAT as well as a soon to be released movie entitled MILES. Kayla is so incredibly thankful to have the opportunity to work with such talented actors as Jared, Rachael and Justin. A humongous special thank you to Jared and Gerry for believing in me and teaching me so much and for all of your hard work in helping me to bring the character Mandy to life! Kayla would also like to thank her parents and brother Ethan for the tremendous support and rides to rehearsals and to all of her family and friends that come out to support the show. Finally, she would like to thank Fearless Productions for enabling the cast of A PROMISE TO YOUR MOTHER to put on this play. Now, Go eat some glue you animals! (Kayla_folz@aol.com)

THE CAST

Justin Remo (Derrek)

Justin is beyond thrilled to work on this project alongside such a talented cast and with the amazing amount of support and guidance that the production team has provided. Justin caught the acting bug having grown up in a theater household. This marks Justin's first principal role having had featured rolls in Fearless Productions THE PILLOWMAN and A SEUSSIFIED CHRISTMAS CAROL. Justin can next be seen performing a featured monologue in SEX, RELATIONSHIPS, and SOMETIMES...LOVE, a Fearless Production opening in December. He would like to dedicate this production to his entire Fearless family and specifically his parents for always allowing him to follow whatever path his footsteps might choose. Justin is represented by Fearless Management and can be contacted at fearlessmgmt@yahoo.com.

THE DIRECTOR

Gerry Appel (Director)

Gerry is excited about this second collaboration with Jared Kelner – the playwright/actor. Back in January of this year, Gerry directed Jared's original play, WHAT DO THEY BECOME? which was selected for the Venus Adonis Theatre Festival. Gerry has been running the Playhouse Acting Academy for the last 5 years following over 40 years as an actor, director and producer. Gerry studied acting at NYU – Tisch School of the Arts, Circle in the Square Theatre School, Catholic University and Montclair State University. Past productions directed include TWIST OF FAITH (an original play), GYPSY, MAME, ONE FLEW OVER THE CUCKOO'S NEST, DEAD MAN'S CELLPHONE, LITTLE SHOP OF HORRORS, FRANKIE AND JOHNNY..., LIPS TOGETHER, TEETH APART, MARY, MARY, ALL IN THE TIMING and several others. Many thanks to this tremendous cast – Jared, Rachel, Kayla and Justin – who continued to make new discoveries with every rehearsal. And, especially, Jared for creating this powerful, layered piece of drama.
(njactingacademy@gmail.com, www.playhouseactingacademy.org)

THE GRAPHIC ARTIST

Chris Orsi (Poster Designer)

Chris is a freelance Graphic Artist and Website Developer. Chris was honored to contribute to this production and wishes the cast and crew of A PROMISE TO YOUR MOTHER a successful run. (corsi617@gmail.com)

SCENES

SCENE 1: Ben's Guidance Counselor office at Madison High School

SCENE 2: School classroom across the hallway from Ben's office

SCENE 3: Ben's Guidance Counselor office at Madison High School

MALCOLM'S INTERLUDE: Somewhere in limbo between heaven and hell in front of his judges

SCENE 4: School classroom across the hallway from Ben's office

SCENE 5: Ben's Guidance Counselor office at Madison High School

SCENE 6: School classroom across the hallway from Ben's office

CHARACTERS

BEN: 40s, High School Guidance Counselor, Malcolm's twin brother, Mandy's uncle.

MANDY: 14, Freshman in High School, Ben's niece.

CELIA: 28, Derrek's mother.

DERREK: 15, Freshman in High School, Celia's son.

MALCOLM: 40s, Ben's twin brother (suggested to be played by the same actor playing BEN).

Written by Jared Kelner
Directed by Gerry Appel

A Fearless Productions Show

2015 Thespis Theater Festival
Hudson Guild Theater
441 W. 26th Street, NY
September 17th & 18th at 6:15pm
September 20th at 8:30pm

PRE-SHOW STAGING:
A single chair, placed DOWNSTAGE CENTER, facing UPSTAGE, sits alone in a pool of red light. Lights fade to begin the show. When the lights come up for Scene 1, this chair is no longer present.

SCENE 1: BEN's Office (STAGE RIGHT) just after the final bell rings at 3:00pm (Desk with phone, folder with papers/reports, 2 chairs (1 UPSTAGE and 1 STAGE LEFT). At LIGHTS UP on the STAGE RIGHT half of the set, BEN is seated behind his desk, reading a report. We hear the sound of a school bell ring and students talking in the hallway as they all exit from their last class. Audio fades as MANDY enters from STAGE RIGHT)

MANDY. Uncle Bennie.

BEN. Hey, Mandy. Come in.

MANDY. Are we leaving soon?

BEN. No. The principal needs me to meet with a new student and his mother. Did you want to take the bus home?

MANDY. No, I'm not taking the bus. I'll just find a classroom and do my homework til you're done.

BEN. OK. Whatever you want.

MANDY. Yeah, that's fine.

BEN. OK. I can talk for a few minutes before they get here, if you want.

MANDY. Um. OK, I guess.

BEN. Good. Come sit. Put down that bag of bricks.

MANDY. I know. It weighs like 50 pounds. It's gonna give me psoriasis.

BEN. You mean scoliosis.

MANDY. Yeah, that.

BEN. So, put some books in your locker. Don't carry them around all day.

MANDY. Everyone picks on the freshman when they're at their lockers.

BEN. Who's picking on you?

MANDY. Nobody. I don't know. People.

BEN. They're picking on you because you're a freshman or because…you know. (PHONE RINGS. BEN picks up the phone) Freshman Guidance Office. Yes, hi. They're in the main office? Yes, that's fine. Send them down. I do. I read them just now. I don't want that to happen either, ma'am. OK. That's fine. I'll see you tomorrow morning. OK. Goodbye. (BEN hangs up the phone). Sorry about that.

MANDY. It's ok. Let me get out of here before they come in.

BEN. Wait. Picking on you. You said people were picking on you. You need to report them.

MANDY. No. I'm not reporting anything. You can't expect people to not talk, Uncle Bennie. It's all over the news. They haven't stopped talking about it for a month.

BEN. Mandy. That is irrelevant. Our family's situation does not give them the right to pick on you. It's none of their business.

MANDY. Are you kidding me? It's everyone's business now.

BEN. Mandy, look, I won't lie to you. This insanity your father created-

MANDY. Why do you do that?

BEN. Do what?

MANDY. Call him "your father?"

BEN. Because he was your father.

MANDY. But he was your brother first and you never call him "your brother." You always say he was "my father." Why can't he just be "your brother?" Why does he have to be "my father?"
BEN. Mandy. None of this is your fault. You need to know that.
MANDY. Uncle Bennie, I'm not blaming myself.
BEN. Good, because you shouldn't. Your father...my brother...whatever the hell Malcolm was and whatever he did, has no bearing on who you are. You're an innocent bystander in all of this and I promise I will do everything I can to protect you. Your mother would have expected that of me and I will honor her memory by being here for you.
MANDY. But everyone is so mean.
BEN. Just try to ignore it.
MANDY. I can't.
BEN. Does it help to know the faculty is just as mean to me?
MANDY. They are?
BEN. They are. The principal, too. They all want me out of here. They don't even make an effort to do it behind my back.
MANDY. What do they say?
BEN. It's not important. Just know that you're not alone in this.
MANDY. Can we move?
BEN. And go where?
MANDY. I hate him.
BEN. I know.
MANDY. (Pause) I love you.
BEN. I love you, too.
MANDY. Are you mad at me?

BEN. About what?
MANDY. Allison.
BEN. Absolutely, not.
MANDY. But she left you.
BEN. Yes, she did.
MANDY. Because of me.
BEN. No.
MANDY. Because you have to watch me now.
BEN. That's ridiculous, Mandy. Come on. Allison did not leave me because of you and you know it. She left me because of Malcolm and because I'm toxic now.
MANDY. You're not toxic.
BEN. Let's not lie to each other, Mandy.
MANDY. When will this be over?
BEN. I wish I knew.
MANDY. I just want it to all go away.
BEN. I know. Are you ok?
MANDY. No. Not really.
BEN. Maybe we should order in something nice for dinner tonight?
MANDY. Maybe. I'm gonna be across the hall. Will you come get me when you're done?
BEN. I promise. (MANDY picks up her backpack and exits STAGE RIGHT. BEN, seated at his desk, looks through the folder of papers. Moments later, CELIA and her son DERREK enter from STAGE RIGHT. DERREK is carrying a heavy backpack.)
CELIA. Mr. Carpenter?

BEN. Yes. Please, come in.

CELIA. Thank you.

BEN. (BEN stands and crosses to greet DERREK and CELIA) You must be Derrek.

DERREK. I guess.

CELIA. Don't start.

DERREK. I didn't say anything.

CELIA. Wipe that smirk off your face.

DERREK. Make me.

CELIA. (To BEN) I'm sorry.

BEN. Don't apologize. No need. Mrs. Minor, it's good to meet you.

CELIA. It's Ms. and yeah, good to meet you, too. Thanks for seeing us.

BEN. Of course. Derrek, I'm Mr. Carpenter, Guidance Counselor for the freshman class.

DERREK. OK, and?

CELIA. I said, "Don't start."

DERREK. Get off my back.

BEN. Derrek, you don't want to be here. I can see that. Look, why don't you go across the hall and do your homework while your mother and I talk. My niece, Mandy, is over there.

CELIA. You're niece is here?

BEN. Yes. She's a freshman too. Derrek, go get settled over there and I'll come get you after your mother and I talk.

DERREK. Why should I?

CELIA. Derrek. Enough. Behave.

DERREK. I said, get off my back.

BEN. Ms. Minor, if I may?

CELIA. Please.

BEN. Thank you. Derrek, you're going to find that I'm good at my job and if you'll let me, I can help you, but my tolerance for behavior like that is very low, especially when it's directed at your mother. So, what's it going to be? Do your homework or go home? Your call.

DERREK. Fine. You win.

BEN. I'm not here to win, Derrek. I'm here to help you. Now, go across the hall, say hi to Mandy, and do your work.

(DERREK exits STAGE RIGHT)

CELIA. Thank you. I am sorry about that.

BEN. Ms. Minor, please don't apologize.

CELIA. OK. And just call me Celia.

BEN. Well, in that case, just call me Ben. Why don't we sit? (BEN sits in the chair behind the desk and CELIA sits in the STAGE LEFT chair)

CELIA. OK. Thank you.

BEN. Of course.

CELIA. Is it wrong that I liked that?

BEN. Liked what?

CELIA. You putting my pain-in-the-ass son in his place.

BEN. Between you and me, no. Sometimes that's all they need. Someone to give it to them straight.

CELIA. I try, but he won't listen to me.

BEN. Does he listen to his father?

CELIA. There is no father.

BEN. Forgive me. May I start over?

CELIA. Please.

BEN. Thank you. OK. Celia, I read Derrek's file. It was missing some information, so please tell me if I have this right. Derrek is 15, but he's a freshman because he was held back one year due to behavior issues.

CELIA. Yes.

BEN. OK. And he was expelled from his last two school due to behavior issues.

CELIA. Yes.

BEN. But you filed appeals both times, moved to different school districts and now Derrek has been here with us at Madison High for 2 weeks.

CELIA. Yes.

BEN. And have you been told specifically why you and Derrek were called in to speak with me today?

CELIA. No, but it doesn't take a genius to figure it out.

BEN. I understand that, but did his teachers or the principal provide specifics?

CELIA. No. The principal called me this morning and told me to meet with you after school today and that you'd let me know what's going on.

BEN. Of course she did. OK. Let me start by saying that what I said to Derrek, about me being good at my job, is true. I've done this for a long time and helping kids is what I was meant to do. Look, the conversation that we're about to have might be difficult, but the more you're willing to share, the easier it will be for me to help Derrek. But, if I cross a line, just tell me and I'll back off. Does that sound fair?

CELIA. Yes, but can I ask you something?
BEN. Of course.
CELIA. Do you really care about these kids?
BEN. Yes.
CELIA. Why?
BEN. Well, I have personal experience with a twin brother who caused a lot of problems growing up and the counselor my parents sent him to was useless. Nothing he said or did helped. Eventually, my brother stopped going and, let's just say, things did not improve. I promised myself that when I grew up, I was going to try to help as many kids as I could. So, here I am.
CELIA. I'm sorry.
BEN. About what?
CELIA. About what your brother put your family through.
BEN. I appreciate that, Celia, very much. OK, let's talk about Derrek.
CELIA. OK.
BEN. Why don't I start by reading the two reports so you understand why you are here? And please know that this is a very small and financially challenged school district. I'm not making excuses. I'm being transparent with you. If we had all of the resources that we truly needed, we'd be having this conversation with the principal, representatives from the Board of Ed and possibly the school's attorney, but unfortunately, things run differently here.
CELIA. That's OK. Just read it.

BEN. This first one is from Mr. Ionuzzo, Derrek's English teacher. *On Thursday at 10:45am, female student Cathy Polusky disrupted class when she stood at her desk, pointed at male student Derrek Minor and screamed "Gross, he's staring at me and playing with himself under the desk." I immediately stopped teaching and brought both students out to the hallway. Cathy restated what she saw. Derrek denied the accusation, claiming he had just come from gym and he felt sweaty around his privates and was simply adjusting himself. Because I did not observe Derrek's behavior firsthand, I let Cathy know I would make sure Principal Stratford was informed. I brought both students back into class and moved Derrek's seat to the opposite side of the room. Class reconvened and ended without further incident.* And that's where it ends.
CELIA. You don't believe him do you?
BEN. Mr. Ionuzzo?
CELIA. No, Derrek.
BEN. He was probably playing with himself in class.
CELIA. But you haven't spoken to him yet. How can you say that?
BEN. Because Derrek does not have Physical Education on Thursdays. Celia, you said it yourself, "It doesn't take a genius to figure it out." I read the reports. I'm making an assumption, but yes, of course, I need to talk to Derrek to understand what happened.
CELIA. OK.

BEN. Why don't I read you the second one now? This one is from Mrs. Wellbeck, one of the cafeteria aides. She's worked at the school for 34 years. *Today at 3rd period lunch, I was at my station by the garbage cans. Sitting where I always sit so I can watch the kids and make sure they're all eating their lunch. The student with Cerebral Palsy, I don't know his name, but he's the one that uses the metal crutches, he was walking to the line to get his food. I saw this other student sitting alone at a table and watching the kid on the crutches come toward him. Then the student at the table took his milk and purposely poured some on the floor to make the poor kid slip and fall. Thank God, I saw it. I ran over and stopped the student on the crutches before he got to the puddle. I helped him around the milk so he didn't slip. When I turned back to yell at the boy who poured the milk on the floor, he was already at the door walking out of the cafeteria. I cleaned up the milk so no one else would get hurt. I asked some of the other students what that boy's name was and they said it was Derrek Minor. I waited until after all the lunches were done and then I wrote this report.*

CELIA. That's horrible. Why would he do that?

BEN. So, that's why you're here.

CELIA. Are you going to expel him?

BEN. That's a possibility, but it's a decision that would be made by many people after many meetings with you, Derrek and everyone involved.

CELIA. I know how it works.

BEN. Celia, are you ok? You look pale.

CELIA. I'm feeling light headed.

BEN. Why don't we take a break? How about a cup of coffee?

CELIA. That would be nice.

(LIHTS FADE OUT on the office)

SCENE 2: Classroom across the hall (STAGE LEFT) (LIGHTS FADE UP on the STAGE LEFT half. There is a long table with 2 chairs behind it facing the audience. MANDY is seated behind the table in the STAGE RIGHT chair doing her homework. DERREK enters from STAGE LEFT with his heavy backpack)

DERREK. Hey.
MANDY. Hi.
DERREK. Are you Mr. What's-his-name's niece?
MANDY. Carpenter and yes.
DERREK. Well he kicked me out and told me I have to stay in here with you.
MANDY. OK, so what do you want from me?
DERREK. I don't want anything from you.
MANDY. Good.
DERREK. Good.
MANDY. What a dick.
DERREK. What did you say?
MANDY. What…a…dick.
DERREK. Nice mouth.
MANDY. Thank you.
DERREK. You're welcome. Can I sit down?
MANDY. Do whatever you want.
DERREK. What's up your ass?
MANDY. Seriously?
DERREK. Whatever. (DERREK sits in the STAGE LEFT chair)
MANDY. (Pause) Why do you have to see my uncle?

DERREK. Cause I'm a bad boy.

MANDY. Is that right.

DERREK. A...bad...boy.

MANDY. What did you do?

DERREK. Wouldn't you like to know?

MANDY. I'm a bad girl sometimes.

DERREK. You are not.

MANDY. How do you know?

DERREK. I can tell.

MANDY. You can't tell anything.

DERREK. Oh yeah, what do you do that's so bad?

MANDY. I'm not telling you.

DERREK. Exactly.

MANDY. Well, I could be if I wanted to.

DERREK. I'm sure you'd be very convincing.

MANDY. I could, too.

DERREK. I'm sure.

MANDY. I smoke cigarettes.

DERREK. I stand corrected. You are a bad, bad girl.

MANDY. Thank you.

DERREK. (Pause) Your uncle, he's a good guy?

MANDY. The best.

DERREK. You think maybe he'll help me?

MANDY. If you let him.

DERREK. It doesn't matter. My mom hates me.

MANDY. How can you say that?

DERREK. Because it's true.

MANDY. You don't know that.

DERREK. And you don't know my mother, so what do you know?

MANDY. You're right. I don't know. Maybe she does hate you. What did you do?

DERREK. I don't want to talk about it.

MANDY. OK. (Pause) You're a freshman?

DERREK. Yeah. How do you know?

MANDY. Cause my uncle's the freshman counselor.

DERREK. Oh.

MANDY. You look older though.

DERREK. I'm 15.

MANDY. And you're only a freshman?

DERREK. Yeah.

MANDY. How come?

DERREK. I got held back.

MANDY. What for?

DERREK. "Behavior Unbecoming" was the official term they used.

MANDY. When?

DERREK. Before.

MANDY. Before when?

DERREK. Before this year.

MANDY. Like in 8th grade?

DERREK. No.

MANDY. Well, when?

DERREK. 4th grade.

MANDY. 4th grade? What did you do?

DERREK. I shit my pants.

MANDY. And they held you back for that?

DERREK. On purpose.

MANDY. What do you mean, "on purpose?"

DERREK. I was bored so I shit my pants.

MANDY. That's disgusting.

DERREK. They made me wear a diaper for a month.

MANDY. In 4th grade?

DERREK. Yup.

MANDY. That's humiliating.

DERREK. Yup.

MANDY. But why did they hold you back for that?

DEREEK. It wasn't just that.

MANDY. What else did you do?

DERREK. I ate the glue.

MANDY. Like the Elmer's glue?

DERREK. A lot of it.

MANDY. That could kill you.

DERREK. How do you know?

MANDY. Because it's glue.

DERREK. And?

MANDY. And it's made with horse hooves or something.

DERREK. It's still good.

MANDY. You're gross.

DERREK. Yup.

MANDY. And what, you still eat it?

DERREK. Yup.

MANDY. And is that why you're here to see my uncle?

DERREK. No.

MANDY. Then why?

DERREK. (Pause) I saw you on the news.

MANDY. Go fuck yourself.

DERREK. Your dad really did all that? To all those young girls?

MANDY. I said, "Go fuck yourself."

DERREK. And he's really dead now? And your mom too?

MANDY. I am not talking to you about this.

DERREK. And that's why you're with your uncle now?

MANDY. I am not here right now.

DERREK. Cause the news, you know, they're full of shit. You can't believe anything they say.

MANDY. I am in my room.

DERREK. But that girl's father really did it, huh? He ran them off the road on purpose?

MANDY. I am safe.

DERREK. Cause your dad raped her?

MANDY. I am safe.

DERREK. And your mom wasn't supposed to be in the car?

MANDY. I am safe.

DERREK. Did your mom know?

MANDY. Get away from me.

DERREK. Calm down.

MANDY. Don't come near me.

DERREK. Calm down.

MANDY. Don't talk about my mother. Ever.

DERREK. I said, calm down.

MANDY. Leave me alone. Why are you here? Why don't you go eat some glue and shit all over yourself, you animal.
DERREK. Watch it.
MANDY. Or what?
DERREK. You don't know me. You don't know anything about me. I could be fucked up just like your father, so watch it.
MANDY. Don't you touch me.
DERREK. Relax. Don't get your panties all bunched up little girl.
MANDY. Why are you so mean?
DERREK. That's a long story. (Lights Fade Out)

SCENE 3: BEN's Office: (As the LIGHTS FADE UP on the STAGE RIGHT half. BEN and CELIA are holding coffee mugs. BEN is seated in the chair behind his desk and CELIA is seated in the STAGE LEFT chair.)

BEN. Your color's back. You feeling a little better?
CELIA. Yes, thank you.
BEN. Should we continue?
CELIA. Yes.
BEN. OK. Remember, if you feel I've crossed a line and you're uncomfortable answering any question, just stop me.
CELIA. Ask whatever you want. I've got nothing to hide.
BEN. OK. Let's start with a few simple questions. Where are you from? Where did Derrek grow up?
CELIA. I grew up in Wingfield, about four hours south. Derrek was born there too.
BEN. Is your family still there?
CELIA. There was no family.
BEN. What do you mean?
CELIA. I grew up in an orphanage.
BEN. OK. I understand. Did you graduate from High School?
CELIA. No.
BEN. Get your G.E.D.?
CELIA. No.
BEN. That's OK. Any interest? I could help you with that?
CELIA. You're a kind man, Ben, but no. That's not important to me anymore.
BEN. I'm sorry to hear that.

CELIA. I'm not. My time has passed. I just want Derrek to have a better life than me.

BEN. You're a good mom.

CELIA. I'm trying to be.

BEN. Are you working?

CELIA. Yes. I'm a waitress at Cornbread's.

BEN. I love it there. That chipotle cornbread is to die for.

CELIA. Yes, it is. I've eaten too much of it apparently.

BEN. Don't be crazy. You're as fit as a fiddle.

CELIA. I wish.

BEN. Maybe next time I go there, you'll be working.

CELIA. I'll bring you some extra cornbread.

BEN. That would be nice.

CELIA. I'm working the dinner shift tonight.

BEN. Maybe my niece and I will stop by.

CELIA. I'd like that.

BEN. So, back to Derrek. A little closer to that line now. You said before that "there is no father."

CELIA. Yes.

BEN. Was there ever a father?

CELIA. No.

BEN. And you were…young, when you had him.

CELIA. Very young.

BEN. Because you look too young to have a 15 year old son.

CELIA. I'm 28.

BEN. (Pause) And his biological father, was he your boyfriend?

CELIA. No.

BEN. Was it planned?

CELIA. No.

BEN. An accidental pregnancy?

CELIA. It was no accident.

BEN. (Pause) I understand. Did you know him?

CELIA. No.

BEN. Did they catch him?

CELIA. He was caught.

BEN. Good. Tell me, why, how were you able to keep Derrek?

CELIA. Well, I wasn't at first. They took him from me and put him in Foster Care for a few years. They only let me see him on weekends, so I dropped out of school. He was supposed to have a better life than me.

BEN. It hasn't been easy, has it?

CELIA. I get by.

BEN. But Derrek, not so much, huh?

CELIA. No. My kid's a mess, but it's not his fault.

BEN. It's not yours either.

CELIA. No? Whose fault is it, yours?

BEN. It's no one's fault. It just is. I can see you feel guilty.

CELIA I'll take that guilt to my grave.

BEN. I wish you wouldn't.

CELIA. You're a good man, Ben.

BEN. Go on now. I'm a work in progress.

CELIA. You did the right thing with your niece.

BEN. Excuse me?

CELIA. Nothing.

BEN. No. What did you just say?

CELIA. Nothing. I didn't say anything.

BEN. What did you just say about my niece?

CELIA. Nothing.

BEN. Celia.

CELIA. I saw you on the news. I saw what happened. I saw you hold Mandy. Protecting her from the cameras. From those vultures. No one ever held me like that. I've never been able to protect Derrek like that. I knew you were a good man, Ben. I moved here for you.

BEN. Moved here for me? Why?

CELIA. So Derrek could go to this school.

BEN. Why?

CELIA. To meet you.

BEN. But why?

CELIA. Why do you think?

BEN. I don't know.

CELIA. Come on, Ben.

BEN. You asked Derrek to do those things? To the girl and the milk?

CELIA. I didn't ask him.

BEN. What?

CELIA. I told him.

BEN. You told him. Why?

CELIA. I saw his picture?

BEN. Derrek's?

CELIA. On the news.

BEN. Whose picture?

CELIA. Malcolm's.

BEN. Malcolm's? What does Malcolm have to do with-
CELIA. I recognized those eyes. That arrogant smirk, how the corner of his lip raised just enough to tell me, "You like that, you little bitch." I saw his picture and then I saw you.
BEN. But when? How?
CELIA. He was working construction at my school. I cut class and went to the bathroom to smoke. He followed me. Told me not to scream, that he wasn't going to hurt me. Said he just wanted a cigarette break. So, I gave him a cigarette and we smoked. He didn't say anything. He just stared at me. I told him I had to get back to class, but he wouldn't let me out. He was a monster and I'm glad he's dead and I'm not sorry I said that. I know he was your brother, but he was an animal and that father of the girl he raped that crashed his car into him, he's a fucking hero in my book. My heart aches for Mandy and her poor mother, but Malcolm got what he deserved and he died like the pig he was....I don't feel good. (LIGHTS OUT FAST)

MALCOLM'S INTERLUDE: As the RED POOL of light comes up, we see the same single chair from the preshow staging placed DOWNSTAGE CENTER, facing UPSTAGE. This time, MALCOLM is sitting on the chair facing the audience, with his chest pressed against the chair's back support.

MALCOLM: (Speaks in a slow, southern drawl directly to the audience) My, oh my. Dear, oh dear. What do we have here? Such a story of tragedy and woe. This poor child. This poor, poor, beautiful child. She's no classic beauty, mind you. She's plain. Simple. But a beauty nonetheless and blah, blah, blah. Forgive me. Where are my manners? I have gotten ahead of myself. Let me rewind so I may henceforth be familiar with ya'll. Allow me the honor, nay the pleasure to introduce myself to you kind, but judgmental people. Believe me, I've seen that look before. There's no reason to avert your eyes, I can feel your *glare* regardless where you *stare* because I am acutely *aware* of the stench in the *air* so I shall rise from this *chair* and begin to *share*. Don't you just love a good rhyme? Children learn so much from a well written rhyme. I know I did. Mother Goose, Dr. Seuss and even Shakespeare rhymed once or deuce. Waterloo, Timbuktu, Maya Angelou, me and you, what to do, what to do, what to do? I suppose I probably look like you expected. Maybe a little grimier, but probably close enough to the distorted picture you created in your dirty little minds. I hope my visage has met your satisfaction. Now, I will say this. I am not from the south, per-say. I am more of a northerly fellow, but there's just something elegant and eerie and haunting about a southern drawl. So to help you understand all about Malcolm, today we shall suspend disbelief and assume I am from the south. Southerly at least. Bayou, Birmingham, Chattanooga, you pick. Makes no difference to me. May I humbly present myself to you...Malcolm Carpenter, at your service. It is a pleasure to make your acquaintance. Especially you and you, sweetheart. Oh yes, I am acutely aware of the cruel joke that my creator has played on me by adorning me with the ironic name, the label, Malcolm Carpenter. I am no fool. I know my fate. My destiny. My purpose in life. Malcolm. Maleficent. Malcontent. Maldoror. The carpenter. The builder. The creator of all things evil in this world. The yin to my brother's yang. The dark to his light. The Tom to his Jerry. Or the Jerry to his Tom. Blah, Blah, Blah. Oh Benjamin. My twin brother. Benjamin. Benevolent. Benefactor. Benvolio. My how you've grown into a fine man. A fine, fine man. Now, as for the charges of sexual impropriety that hang like a prickly noose around my callous neck, I can only say this. Guilty as charged. But only for the ones where I was present. And this woman here, I do not recall. I can look you in the eye and say with certainty that I was not present for this indiscretion that has been laid upon her. Now that does not mean I was not (Pointing down to reference a physical location) present. What it means is that I was not (pointing to his head) present. And when one is not (Pointing to his head) present, one cannot, should not, will not be held accountable for one's actions. However, if it is proved, or proven, by some means biological, familial, then I will substantiate, corroborate, and commiserate as I stand at the *gate* to hear my *fate* that I made her once my *mate* on that most unfortunate *date*. And so the trees turn green and the grass turns green, but the trees turn green first, why? Because of all the foliage spill and so you see, my faithful friends, we have come to the point in the story where you learn why. Why old Malcolm here was the way I was, is the way I is and will forever be the way I will be throughout eternity. I do believe another rhyme shall do the trick. The story of a little boy who went click, click, click. (Pause) There once was an old man named MacFee who dwelt in a dwelling close to me, me, me. The kids in town called him Mr. Mac, Mac, Mac. And oh boy did Mr. Mac have a knack, knack, knack for finding just the right boy, boy, boy to gently mold into his toy, toy, toy. One day walking home when I was six, six, six, kicking rocks and throwing sticks, sticks, sticks, Mr. Mac called to me, "Boy, boy, boy, come upon my porch for a toy, toy, toy." So I skipped and I bounded right up to Mr. Mac, Mac, Mac and put out my hand like a druggard yearns for his crack, crack, crack. Mr. Mac said, "Sit on my lap, lap, lap. You look tired boy, rest a spell and take a nap, nap, nap." His boney fingers brushed up and down my arm, arm, arm. He said, "Relax boy, I won't do you no harm, harm, harm." So I closed my eyes, eyes, eyes, and told myself lies, lies, lies. And from that day on, there was no going back, back, back, thanks to good old Mr. Mac, Mac, Mac. (Pause) Perhaps now you fine looking people have gained a certain perspective on things. Now I know this does not excuse my actions. I own them all. And I suppose even the ones that I was not (Pointing to his head) present for. But alas, I must bid you adieu, a bon voyage, a fair-the-well, a toot-a-loo. My time here is done. Goodbye. (As MALCOLM walks off STAGE RIGHT dragging his chair behind him, he pauses and looks at one woman in the audience, winks and smirks) Well aren't you something. (MALCOLM exits. LIGHTS OUT)

SCENE 4: Classroom across the Hall (LIGHTS UP on the STAGE LEFT half. MANDY and DERREK are sitting on the table at opposite ends from each other)

DERREK. Your name's Mandy, right?
MANDY. Yes.
DERREK. Is that short for something? Like Amanda?
MANDY. What do you care?
DERREK. I'm just asking.
MANDY. Don't.
DERREK. I said I was sorry. I didn't think you were going to freak out like that.
MANDY. Well, don't talk about things that are none of your business.
DERREK. Alright. I won't. (Pause) My name's Derrek, by the way.
MANDY. Is that short for something? Like Derrek-crapped-his-pants?
DERREK. Hey.
MANDY. Or Derrek-can't-stop-eating-glue.
DERREK. Ha Ha.
MANDY. (Pause) I'm sorry.
DERREK. It's ok. I get it. (Pause) So, you never have?
MANDY. What? Crapped in my pants on purpose?
DERREK. No. Only I do shit like that. I mean tasted glue.
MANDY. No. No way.
DERREK. You want to?
MANDY. No.

DERREK. Cause I have a bottle in my bag.

MANDY. You carry a bottle of glue with you?

DERREK. Yeah. I get hungry sometimes.

MANDY. You're weird, you know that?

DERREK. But you like it, right?

MANDY. No.

DERREK. Come on. You know you find me-

MANDY. Repulsive.

DERREK. Irresistible.

MANDY. You wish.

DERREK. (Pause) So, your uncle, what's his name?

MANDY. Benjamin. Ben

DERREK. Ben?

MANDY. Yes.

DERREK. Uncle Ben?

MANDY. Yes.

DERREK. Uncle Ben?

MANDY. Yes.

DERREK. Like the rice?

MANDY. No, not like the rice. Like the uncle.

DERREK. His name is Uncle Ben.

MANDY. His name is not Uncle Ben. I just call him Uncle Ben. Bennie. You're an idiot.

DERREK. I bet if we put some glue on Uncle Ben's rice it would taste good.

MANDY. Like risotto.

DERREK. Like risotto.

MANDY. This is the stupidest conversation I've ever had.

DERREK. But you're in a better mood now, right?

MANDY. I guess.

DERREK. That's all that matters.

MANDY. (Pause) It's from a song.

DERREK. What is?

MANDY. My name, Mandy.

DERREK. It is?

MANDY. Yeah. From some piano guy my mom listened to when she was a kid.

DERREK. What's it about?

MANDY. I don't know exactly, but there's a line about this one kiss that makes him stop shaking. I've always liked the idea that a kiss could have that much power. Like one kiss from the right guy could stop me from shaking.

DERREK. Or one kiss from you could maybe save him.

MANDY. Yeah. Maybe that too.

DERREK. Have you kissed a guy yet?

MANDY. I'm not telling you.

DERREK. That's ok. You don't have to.

MANDY. What's taking them so long anyway? I thought you said they were talking for a few minutes and then were going to come get you.

DERREK. I did. I guess I really screwed up this time.

MANDY. What did you do?

DERREK. It doesn't matter. They're going to expel me…again.

MANDY. Again?

DERREK. Three times a charm.

MANDY. Why are you like this?

DERREK. Lack of parental supervision, I've been told.

MANDY. Seriously. Why?

DERREK. Got any cigarettes?

MANDY. Maybe.

DERREK. Can I get one?

MANDY. Will you tell me what you did?

DERREK. Maybe.

MANDY. But you can't smoke in here.

DERREK. Why not?

MANDY. Don't be stupid. (MANDY takes a box of cigarettes out of her bag and hands DERREK a cigarette)

DERREK. Alright, I'll save it for later. Thanks. (DERREK puts the cigarette into his backpack)

MANDY. Yep.

DERREK. (Pause) I never have, either.

MANDY. What?

DERREK. Kissed a girl. I mean a real kiss.

MANDY. You haven't?

DERREK. No.

MANDY. Maybe you're not such a bad boy after all.

DERREK. Maybe. (LIGHTS FADE OUT)

SCENE 5: BEN's Office: (LIGHTS FADE UP on the STAGE RIGHT half. BEN has pulled his chair out from behind his desk and is now sitting STAGE LEFT of CELIA)

BEN. Celia, maybe we should stop. You don't look well, again.
CELIA. I'll be ok, Ben.
BEN. You sure?
CELIA. Yes. You're the first person I have ever told.
BEN. Ever?
CELIA. The whole story at least. The truth.
BEN. What my brother did to you was inexcusable.
CELIA. Yes.
BEN. What can I do to help you?
CELIA. Derrek.
BEN. You want me to get Derrek?
CELIA. I want you to help Derrek.
BEN. Of course.
CELIA. Like Mandy.
BEN. Whatever you need.
CELIA. Whatever Derrek needs. It's not about me.
BEN. Of course. I meant whatever you need me to do to help you, help Derrek, I will.
CELIA. I can't help him.
BEN. Yes, you can.
CELIA. I need you to be there for him, Ben.
BEN. I promise.
CELIA. He has no idea about any of this.
BEN. Of course not.

CELIA. And he can never know the truth.

BEN. You have my word.

CELIA. (Pause) What happens next about the reports?

BEN. I'll take care of it tomorrow.

CELIA. You can make it all go away.

BEN. No. Not go away, but I know what to do to make sure he's ok.

CELIA. What will you do?

BEN. Don't worry about that now. I'll take care of it.

CELIA. And you promise to look after him?

BEN. I promise.

CELIA. And if anything should happen to me?

BEN. Like what?

CELIA. I don't know. But if one day something happens to me, I get hurt, or die or just disappear?

BEN. That's not going to happen.

CELIA. But if it did? Would you make sure he's safe?

BEN. Yes.

CELIA. And loved?

BEN. Why are you talking like this?

CELIA. I'm just tired.

BEN. (Pause) Look, these people have it out for me here anyway, so what the hell. I have an idea. Why don't we all go back to my house, the four of us? I'll cook dinner and we can talk. We won't have to tell Derrek everything, but maybe, in a safer place, maybe he'll open up? What do you say?

CELIA. It sounds...perfect. But I have to work tonight.

BEN. Take the night off.

CELIA. I need the money.

BEN. (BEN takes out his wallet and pulls out some bills) Here's $83. Take the night off.

CELIA. It's too much.

BEN. For what my brother did to you, it will never be enough. Take it, please.

CELIA. (CELIA takes the money) Thank you. But I have to go to the restaurant and tell my manager in person that I can't work tonight. He'll understand if I tell him in person. He won't believe me if I do it over the phone.

BEN. OK. Derrek can come home with Mandy and me if you're comfortable with that. Then you can meet me at my house.

CELIA. Would you do that?

BEN. Yes. I'll take the kids home. Go talk to your manager, then come over.

CELIA. I may be a while.

BEN. That's ok. They'll help me get dinner started.

CELIA. That will be a first.

BEN. What's that?

CELIA. A family dinner.

BEN. (BEN writes his address on a piece of paper and hands it to CELIA) Here's my address.

CELIA. What are you going to tell him?

BEN. That I'm here for him and that I'll talk to his teachers and the principal for him. That I'll vouch for him, for what it's worth, but that it's not a one way street. He's got to make an effort. It'll be tough, but he can do it.

CELIA. Thank you, Ben.

(LIGHTS FADE OUT)

SCENE 6: Classroom across the Hall (LIGHTS UP on the STAGE LEFT. MANDY and DERREK are sitting on top of the table next to each other)

DERREK. Are you sure you want to do this?
MANDY. I think so.
DERREK. Cause you don't have to if you don't want to.
MANDY. No, I want to.
DERREK. OK. Give me your hand. (DERREK squirts a small drop of glue into MANDY'S palm). There.
MANDY. Do I lick it?
DERREK. If you want. Or dip your finger in and taste it.
MANDY. How do you do it?
DERREK. Me? I just squirt it into my mouth.
MANDY. You do not.
DERREK. No, really I do.
MANDY. I don't believe you. (DERREK squirts some glue into his mouth) Oh, my god! That's disgusting!
DERREK. No, it's not. Try it.
MANDY. I'm scared.
DERREK. I thought you were a bad girl.
MANDY. Fine. (MANDY licks the glue off her hand) Eeeeewwww. It's tangy. Why is it tangy?
DERREK. It's amazing, right?
MANDY. No. It's disgusting.
DERREK. But good, right?
MANDY. No. There's nothing good about it. It's gross. What do I do?

DERREK. Spit it out.

MANDY. Where?

DERREK. Here. (DERREK pulls a t-shirt out of his backpack and holds it out for MANDY to spit into. MANDY spits out the glue into the t-shirt repeatedly until it's all gone.)

MANDY. Why did you make me do that?

DERREK. I didn't make you do anything, Mandy. You asked.

MANDY. Yeah, but you should've stopped me.

DERREK. Why would I do that?

MANDY. Because my tongue is melting. Is it all gone?

DERREK. I don't know. Stick it out. (DERREK uses the t-shirt to wipe MANDY'S tongue, then crumples the t-shirt and shoves it into his backpack) There. All clean.

MANDY. Disgusting.

DERREK. So, how was that?

MANDY. I'd rather eat a cigarette.

DERREK. That's disgusting.

MANDY. That's disgusting?

DERREK. Yes.

MANDY. No, that would be like candy.

DERREK. Candy, huh?

MANDY. Yes.

DERREK. (DERREK takes out the cigarette from his jacket) Want to try?

MANDY. No. (DERREK replaces the cigarette)

DERREK. You have some glue on your lip.

MANDY. Get it off. I'm shaking. (DERREK gently wipes this glue from MANDY'S lip with his finger and slowly leans in to kiss her. MANDY does not pull away. They share an innocent kiss for a few seconds that calms them both. She stops shaking. They pull apart just a bit so they can look in each other's eyes and acknowledge the power of this one kiss. BEN and CELIA enter from STAGE LEFT)

BEN. Hey! What are you doing? (DERREK and MANDY jump off the table and move to opposite sides of the room)

MANDY. Nothing. We were just talking.

DERREK. Yeah. We were just talking.

CELIA. It didn't look like talking to me.

DERREK. Well it was, mom. Relax.

BEN. OK. None of that. You are never allowed to do that again.

MANDY. We were just talking, Uncle Bennie. I promise.

DERREK. Yeah, Uncle Bennie.

CELIA. Derrek!

DERREK. Mom!

BEN. OK. Everyone, just calm down.

DERREK. I'm calm. You calm?

BEN. Yes, I'm calm.

DERREK. Mom, you calm?

CELIA. Yes.

DERREK. Mandy?

MANDY. I'm calm.

DERREK. See Ben, everyone's calm. You're calm, they're calm, I'm calm. We're all calm.

BEN. Good. Let's all just stay calm.

DERREK. Is it my turn now, Ben? Do I get to explain how my junk was all sweaty from gym?

MANDY. What?

DERREK. Nothing.

BEN. No, Derrek. Actually, your mother and I have another idea.

DERREK. Is that right, mom? You have an idea?

BEN. Derrek, I'm here to help you.

DERREK. Really?

BEN. Yes.

DERREK. And why is that?

BEN. Because I made a promise to your mother.

DERREK. And why would you do that?

BEN. I have my reasons.

DERREK. You some kind of pervert?

CELIA. Enough. That is enough out of you. This man is offering you a lifeline out of the kindness of his heart. For reasons you cannot begin to understand, he is offering to help you, so show some respect and shut your damn mouth.

(CELIA takes a deep breath. Pause.) Whoooh! That felt good!

BEN. Derrek, you're going to come back to my house with Mandy and me.

MANDY. What?

DERREK. Why?

CELIA. For dinner.

DERREK. Why?

BEN. So we can talk in a more relaxed environment.

DERREK. And what about you, mom? You're not coming?
BEN. Your mother needs to go to work and tell her manager that she's taking the night off. Then she'll come over and we'll all sit down for dinner. After that, we'll talk about what we all need to do to help you get back on track.
DERREK. Is that right, mom? Is that the plan?
CELIA. Mmm, Hmm.
DERREK. So you're going to go to work and then come over to Uncle Ben's?
CELIA. Mmm, Hmm.
DERREK. (Pause) OK. Can we have risotto?
BEN. I don't think I have rice.
DERREK. Seriously?
MANDY. Let's pick some up on the way home.
BEN. That sounds like a plan. (To CELIA) You've got my address?
CELIA. Mmm, Hmm.
BEN. See you soon, Ms. Minor.
CELIA. Yeah.
BEN. OK, kids, grab your bags of bricks and let's get out of here. (MANDY and DERREK pick up their backpacks. BEN exits STAGE LEFT, followed by MANDY)
CELIA. (Just as DERREK reaches the STAGE LEFT door) Derrek. (DERREK stops and turns to CELIA)
DERREK. What?
CELIA. I...
DERREK. What? (Pause) Spit it out.
CELIA. I love you, very much.

DERREK. (With a smirk on his face) Well aren't you something. (DERREK exits. CELIA is standing alone on stage DOWNSTAGE CENTER. A red SPOTLIGHT surrounds her and out of the shadows from the back enters MALCOLM. He stands a few feet UPSTAGE and at an angle to CELIA, just at the edge of the SPOTLIGHT. We see CELIA struggling with following through with the agreed upon plan for dinner or leaving her son in BEN's care, never to return. No decision is made and the audience should be left to decide for themselves what CELIA decided to do)
(LIGHTS OUT)
THE END

SET DESIGN

BEN'S OFFICE: Office desk, 2 chairs, 2 or 3 "Guidance Counselor" posters about SAT Prep, Bullying, Smoking, Alcohol/Drug Awareness

CLASSROOM: Long table, 2 chairs, 2 or 3 science related posters (Biology, Evolution)

MALCOM'S INTERLUDE: 1 chair (1 of the chairs from BEN's Office should be used)

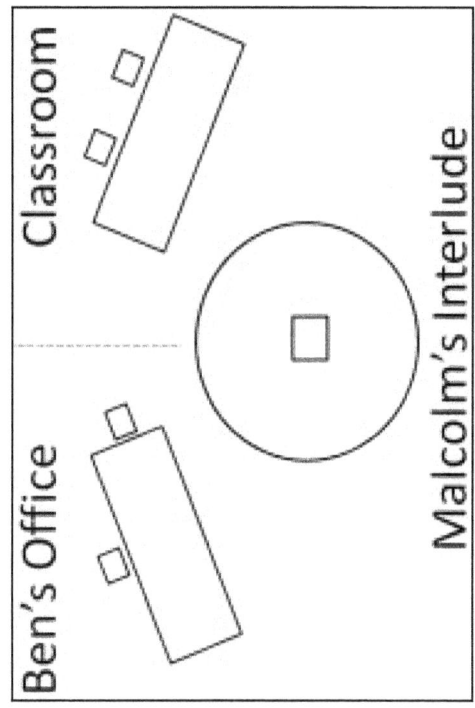

COSTUMES

BEN: Khaki pants, brown shoes, brown socks, brown belt, long-sleeve solid color button-down shirt

MANDY: Black leggings, bagging sweater (dark colors), black socks, simple black shoes

CELIA: "Cornbread's Uniform" Black leggings, short-sleeve bright-color "uniform-like" shirt, black socks, black tennis shoes (Keds)

DEREK: Distressed jeans, white socks, black sneakers, black t-shirt (no logos), grey zipper-hoodie

MALCOLM: Distressed dark pants, white socks, old work boots, white distressed tank-top undershirt, Fake damaged buck-teeth (See www.drbukk.com)

PROPS LIST

BEN
1 folder with 2 reports (Derrek's file and extra pages inside)
1 Desk phone
1 Pen/Pencil Holder with Pens & Pencils
1 Pad of scrap paper
2 coffee mugs
1 Wallet with $83 dollars
1 Cellular phone

CELIA
Shoulder strap bag full with wallet, make-up, keys, etc

MANDY
1 backpack full of books
1 Box of cigarettes

DERREK
1 backpack full of books
1 Bottle of Elmer's glue
1 White T-shirt or rag

MALCOLM
1 Zippo lighter with evil image

SOUND CUES

Original production music can be downloaded at www.jaredkelner.com

PRE-SHOW MUSICS
Ominous music plays from the moment the house is open until the lights fade just before Scene 1.

SCENE 1
As lights come up and we see BEN at his desk. School bell rings and we hear sounds of high school students in the hallways after school is over. Sound fades as MANDY enters.

4 digital telephone rings just after BEN's line "They're picking on you because you're a freshman or because...you know."

MALCOLM'S INTERLUDE
Ominous music, same as Pre-Show music, to be played low under MALCOLM'S monologue.

SCENE 6
Ominous music, same as Pre-Show music, to be played as the red spot light fades on CELIA.

LIGHTING CUES

PRE-SHOW
Pool of red light on a lone chair DOWNSTAGE CENTER

SCENES 1, 3, 5 (BEN's OFFICE)
BEN'S office, STAGE RIGHT, is fully lit and the Classroom, STAGE LEFT, is in darkness. Lights momentarily fade to darkness between scenes.

SCENES 2, 4, 6 (THE CLASSROOM)
The Classroom, STAGE LEFT, is fully lit and BEN'S office, STAGE RIGHT, is in darkness. Lights momentarily fade to darkness between scenes.

MALCOLM'S INTERLUDE
A red pool of light on the DOWNSTAGE CENTER chair and MALCOLM. Both BEN'S office and the Classroom are in darkness.

FINAL MOMENTS OF SCENE 6
After DERREK exits, lights cross-fade to the red pool of light DOWNSTAGE CENTER. Both BEN'S office and the Classroom are in darkness. Fade to black.

CURTAIN CALL
Full lights up

Written by Jared Kelner
Directed by Gerry Appel

A Fearless Productions Show

2015 Thespis Theater Festival
Hudson Guild Theater
441 W. 26th Street, NY
September 17th & 18th at 6:15pm
September 20th at 8:30pm

For Performance Inquires
Contact Jared Kelner
jared@jaredkelner.com

To watch a video of the original
cast performance, visit
www.jaredkelner.com

www.ingramcontent.com/pod-product-compliance
Lightning Source LLC
Chambersburg PA
CBHW071415040426
42444CB00009B/2262